T0365290

A LITTLE SLICE OF HEAVEN

by
Ruthie

Channeled

by
Liz

Notes

by
Donna

Order this book online at www.trafford.com
or email orders@trafford.com

Most Trafford titles are also available at major online book retailers.

Print information available on the last page.

ISBN: 978-1-4120-5801-8 (sc)
ISBN: 978-1-4122-3596-9 (e)

Trafford rev. 11/28/2023

 www.trafford.com
North America & international
toll-free: 844-688-6899 (USA & Canada)
fax: 812 355 4082

I would like to dedicate this book
to my grandmother Elizabeth Lehman.
My grandmother had a lot of love in her heart and
shared that love with many.

ACKNOWLEDGEMENTS

To my children Bobby and Leigh, thank you for being in my life and for your love and support. You give my life meaning, and without you I would only be a shell. A special thank you to my daughter Leigh for the cover.

To my granddaughter Emily, who loves rainbows, you are my rainbow.

I would like to acknowledge my mother who helped me introduce Ruthie to the world, and who taught me strength.

To Lucille who called Ruthie "A Little Slice of Heaven." She is now with Ruthie on the other side.

Thelma Roberts and Bea Edmunds, thank you for taking the time to help with proof-reading of my book.

This book would not have been possible without the help and support of my dear friend Donna Rybovic. She has devoted her time to the typing, editing, and promoting A Little Slice of Heaven, thank you for all your hard work.

I would like to acknowledge all the wonderful people I have met while working with Ruthie for allowing us to come into their lives.

CONTENTS

PREFACE

A spirit named Ruthie channeled the following pages through Liz. The words of Ruthie are her facts and visions. The following pages have been written over a period of years. This has been put into book form so others can benefit from it.

When a spirit speaks, they give communication in short and brief sentences. What is important to a mortal may not be important to a spirit.

All the information that was given by Ruthie was recorded and then put to type. Some words were changed in order for the public to have a better understanding of her writing.

I hope you will enjoy and understand that Ruthie is a spirit that came to teach and allow you to make your own choices and have your own beliefs.

With Love,
Liz

THE BLANKET

When you look at life and the person you have become, we sometimes wonder if that's all we can be, or if we change, would it be good for others and ourselves? We begin to select things, dream of things, and hope for anything to give an answer to what this life is.

Life is like a blanket, and no matter what you select, the blanket is yours and it will last. You must take care of your blanket and the blanket will keep you from the cold, hide you when you feel the need not to show, comfort you, you can have fun on the blanket, rest and so on.

A life has as much for all, but if you lay all your energy down and wait for the answer, it would be like taking the blanket and putting it down, standing over it, and never feeling what kind of blanket it is. There are many beautiful blankets, don't let yours go to waste, use it everyday, and move it about.

Love to all,
Ruthie

PRELUDE

Many have little understanding of the voices and thoughts we receive, we know we hear it, and dream it, yet is it spirit? Some may have their own theory, some will ignore it completely. I'm not sure of all the answers, one thing I can tell you, we are not alone, and it is not make-believe. Whether you are a child or an adult, you have a friend near you and that friend is spirit.

We are not always sure why spirit comes to us and we might not have an understanding of the process, but what you are about to read will give you an insight on why spirits come, the work they do, and why they select mortals to help them.

A LITTLE SLICE OF HEAVEN

THE COMING OF RUTHIE

Would you make the choice to discover more about your life and others? There are some that would say no, maybe out of fear, thinking that life is a set plan. Maybe you're a person like myself that rides the middle of the road waiting for things to come, hoping for the best. Then there are the ones that feel they have all the answers about life, and have no need to understand the next person and why things happen. Some know there is a choice in life, yet they will want another person to make that choice for them. The word choice is a frightening word; it means if you're wrong, or even right, you take the responsibility of the choice you made. But what if you make a choice and are unaware you made that choice, like getting lost on a trip and finding a place you love, or selecting an item because you liked it, and than you find out you need a present for someone. Maybe you selected this book, not sure why, but you were drawn to it subconsciously. You might even choose to take on a new and different life and not even realize it until it happens. It's funny how the unconscious choices we make can change our lives, and end up teaching us and giving us the most joy.

When you're young you make a lot of unconscious decisions, some might call them dreams, or ideas, but whatever you want to call them, they take us to the next level. I wanted to be a writer once. As the years passed, I never thought I would actually write a book, and I certainly never thought that the subject matter would somehow involve my life. Little did I know that in time, my life would change and veer down a path with a more noble aspiration. Although this may seem egotistical, I really do believe that when you help others you are choosing a more noble direction. The statement may seem self-centered, but my life is nowhere close to that. When I help a person I become part of their life, I begin to relate to their path in life, and an understanding grows between us.

My unconscious life-altering experience started twenty years ago when Ruthie first introduced herself to me. I could hear someone but I couldn't see anyone. What do you do in that situation? Well, I'll tell you, I just laughed to myself and ignored it. The next couple of days, strange things began to happen. I'm not trying to scare you; this isn't poltergeist all over again. The hair dryer would turn on and off and things were moved out of place, because Ruthie was letting me know that she was here to stay. I humored myself because no one was around and I asked, "Who you are?" I was immediately told, "A spirit."

My first thought was that I'm really losing it. I asked

what that meant. Again, she answered immediately, as if she was waiting to be asked, she replied, "I am from Christ's light." I assumed this meant that there was no need to fear for my safety but I still wasn't sure what was transpiring. She explained to me that she was here to work through me to teach love. I told her she picked the wrong person to work with. I'm not a teacher and I wasn't sure if I wanted to take on a situation like this at this time in my life.

I asked what I should call her, she announced, "Gertomp." I was not sure of that name, so I asked her where and why she chose that name. She informed me it was a spiritual name. She told me I could call her Ruth Theresa Spoons. This was a name she had in the 1800's, when we were friends. Over the years, that name turned into Ruthie. I started asking her questions that lasted into the night about what she expected of me. She explained that during the operation that took place a few weeks prior, I had crossed over, meaning something happened during the operation. It made sense because I had lost a lot of blood and my doctor was surprised I pulled through. The tumor I had removed was larger than they expected, and I was very weak. While the operation was being performed, I crossed over and Ruthie asked me to work with her in exchange for my life. I don't remember agreeing to this, but it must have happened because she is here and I'm a different person. Ruthie returned with me and the inner soul that filled my body. I will go into greater detail

about inner and outer souls in Chapter 2. She explained
that this is how we will be able to communicate with each
other. Her purpose here ultimately was to help others and
to teach people to love. Part of my soul was sacrificed, and
I use the word sacrifice because my life has never been the
same. Now instead of going shopping or spending time
with my family and friends, I am working with people and
doing readings, which is a word used to describe the ses-
sions I have with my clients. I sit down and relax and allow Ruthie to channel her thoughts and her voice into my
head.

Over the years I asked Ruthie about herself and how
the decision came about to come to this world and work
with me. I know she told me that she needed to help
and teach, but I wanted to know the process making that
decision. We all know that we will pass over, and have
been told about Heaven or a place on the other side, and
we all have questions about the other side. So I thought
this would be the perfect time to get a few answers to my
questions. When I asked her about the process, she told
me she elected to take on this job. I told her I understood
that, and I asked her to explain it to me in more detail so
I would have a complete understanding, by giving it to me
in a visual view, along with words. What I saw and heard
that day helped me to understand and want to work with
Ruthie.

She described a family, who she was with when she
elected to take on the job of teacher. She went on to tell

me that she wanted to teach and to help a number of souls and not just one. Even though she works with me, she is able to touch many souls. When she elected to do this she knew she would be separated from her spiritual family, but it was okay. She explains that when you take on an assignment it gives you spiritual growth, plus it is a way to be with mortals without completely becoming a mortal. I was shown a group of souls, Ruthie being one of them, agreeing to find a person and work with that person for some time. This wasn't conversed through words, but like a dream. I knew what was going on, and felt their thoughts. Ruthie informed me that taking on a job is a simple process by making a decision, planning where you will go, and selecting a person to do the job with. Other energies along with Ruthie knew that the mortal world had a need to learn more about love and feel love.

A group of ten was asked to spread themselves throughout the world. They needed to select a person who was about to die, and who would be willing to agree to work with the spirits. They decided that they would not switch souls with the mortal, but would work with the outer part of our souls, giving the body energy through the subconscious mind, until we were able to adjust to the inner part of the soul that was given in replacement. She told me that the group of ten spiritual souls, one being Ruthie, gathered and selected different areas of the world in which to work. They might use a different technique than Ruthie, but they will get their point across to the world.

She tells me that you are not selected for this type of job based upon your life experiences or levels of knowledge in spiritual world; you are the soul in charge of picking the job. When the time comes to communicate to the mortal, the spirit surrounds the mortal soul during the operation or passing, and offers the mortal the choice. During the crossing, the soul is communicated with and asked if they are willing to join the spirit in teaching life's lessons. Ruthie informed me that she returns to the other side and reveals what she has done with the souls she works with. She says she is not graded in any way, but must show that she is continuing on with the teaching. She and the others know they must stay within the guidelines and not take away a person's free will. The review is done by other souls that gather to witness each soul that has a job like this one. They are not on a higher level, only doing their job; they do have knowledge and might take on a position to help the soul that has come here, like Ruthie.

I have been asked over the years, why me? Why not someone else? I asked her this question, and her answer was simple. She needed to complete a task, and to do this she needed a mortal to work with. She told me that we shared past lives together as friends, and that she chose me because we would work well together. She said we had an understanding that stems back over many years, and this understanding and trust would help others. I know that I agreed to this deal because of my family. I was a young woman with small children and a husband.

I wasn't ready to give up my life and move on to the other side. Now, twenty years later, I'm thankful that I did agree.

I guess you can say I am a minority. In many ways I stand out from the average person. Some call this a gift. I look at this gift as a job. Being a psychic, you develop a reputation and many times you find you are defending the good you do for others. I know that what I do can be scary. It was scary to me at first, but everything in life can be scary if you close your mind and say that it is impossible. Some might chose not to believe in what I do and that is fine, but I only wish they could stand on my spot and have understanding, as I understand them. This doesn't mean I want them to change; I just want them to know that what I'm doing is for the good, not bad.

I have been asked why Ruthie waited until now to put her words on paper. I can answer that question myself. I now understand that I needed to learn more about spirits, their work, and Ruthie herself. I have been told that I'm lucky to have her with me, to help me with my life. What they don't understand is that Ruthie will give me guidance, but she is not able to enhance my life. I need to experience and understand others and their situations. She showed me how a spirit can heal pain and strengthen the soul. She taught me not to judge a person by their skin or their thoughts, but to look a little deeper into their soul. Many times what we see or hear is not all a person is. She shared her thoughts of the mortal life with me, and showed me that fear is only a sadness that is not required in life. I have more understanding of death now, and know first-hand that the ones we love are always near us, even if we cannot see them. The one gift she has given to me is her friendship, for she has shown me that spirits are around all of us, and that spirits are willing to guide us if we are willing to ask for guidance. I must say that Ruthie gives me many laughs and happiness. Spirits hold no baggage, pain, or judgment. They speak in short sentences, yet they deliver clear thoughts. We as mortals need to listen. As Ruthie has said many times, take a moment and touch someone. We all have a spiritual soul around us. It could be a past friend as Ruthie was to me, or a family member. They make clear what can be a fog to us on this level. As for me, I look at it as a comfort and a protection, which is something we can all use in our lives.

So you see her job began with showing me that we are more than a mortal body and that the soul of a person has significant importance. We connect to each other and need each other, and we should take time to understand each other.

The next chapters are Ruthie's words that she related to me over the years to share with others. I hope her words will give you an insight not only in your life, but also into life on the other side.

SPIRITS

Why are spirits here?

They are here to help people.

Are they always here?

Sometimes, but sometimes they are in spiritual world.

What is a spirit?

The word spirit means energy of the soul.

What is a soul?

The best definition I can give would be who you really are as a person. If you look at yourself from the outside in, you will find you have a soul. This soul is one body of energy, but it has two separate functions. I know everyone views the soul as solid energy that flows throughout the human body. My explanation is the same; only I will break it down so you will understand.

I refer to the body of the soul as the inner soul and outer soul. Sometimes the soul can be referred to as high energy or low energy, however, the term strong versus weak has also been used. No matter how you refer to the soul, it is one body of energy.

The inner part of the soul is connected to the brain and

the heart. The brain works as the computer sending information to the heart, which works like fuel. This information is broken down into segments, and a portion of these segments turns into emotions.

The outer part of your soul works with your subconscious mind, your personality, your features, and your skin texture. It will also have control of your memory and your dreams. The outer part of the soul controls when you hear those little voices, when you feel things, and when you bring back communication from your dreams. Memory is the energy, or brain waves, that the soul has no need to keep. The inner and outer parts of the soul combined gives the body a complete energy.

So when you think of spirit, understand that it is a living energy protected by skin that works in two different sections. Knowing this is energy, you will also understand that this energy can move, think, breathe, and communicate. It is a living art form.

A good spirit will come to bring love and understanding. They will stay, and they will give you help, like a watchdog. Can a spirit change a situation in your life? No, but if you ask for help, they will give you the clarity so you can solve the problem.

Now let's look at what happens when you leave the body and the soul releases. The inner part of the soul will go first; it will rise above the body. The soul will also rise above the body if a soul is in a coma or dream state. The inner part of the soul will follow whoever comes for them into the energy of love. The outer part of the soul will follow the inner soul. This is why a person will become cold when death happens. The emotional part leaves the body first. After you return to spiritual world and while in the rest area, you will relinquish what is stored in the subconscious mind.

The communication then will be filed away. The brain itself stays with the body and will deteriorate with the body. The information you take back to the other side is for the soul to look back on. This information is stored until the soul has a need to use or share with other souls, and even mortals. This is why a lot of times when you come back into a life you will remember certain things. When you return to a mortal life, you might bring this information back with you. Some things might be well known. You might remember a place or feel you know someone at first sight. This information will also help you as a guide. If a soul needs assistance and the guide is not familiar with the situation, the guide can review past lives, so they can give aid.

You might want to talk to your guides. Some wait for a voice, although spirits can work through many forms. They will work with electrical equipment in your home or wherever. Lights will go on and off, bells might ring. There could be a flash of energy that will pass by you, or even a shadow. This could be spirits that are around you. Some might feel a chill or cool air. They love to work with telephones, that energy is a strong link. Spirits want you to know they are close and want to help. The thoughts they give you could save your life or put you back on track.

A spiritual guide will do many jobs to help everyone in the world. They look over the whole world, and all of its concerns. There are people with so many difficulties and issues; these spirits have the ability to help.

There are spirits that will work to keep peace and to help during wartime. Spirits can be found in hospitals, schools, government, roadways, churches, and homes helping people and giving comfort. Wherever a person will be, spirits may be there. They are not here watching every movement you make, for this would take a great deal of energy. A spirit will assist with the important things in your life, for it takes a lot of energy to communicate out to a mortal. If only a mortal would take the time to understand and connect, then spirit and human life can be a complete circle of love.

Here on the Earth you come to be with someone you can help, teach, or learn from. When you pass on and no longer have skin, and become a spirit you can remain with your family and give guidance. Spirits will come with different titles, as in angels, guides, ghosts, fairies, and ears. They are all spirits but will have different jobs.

Are there bad spirits?

"Yes, there are." Some people have asked if I am a bad spirit. "No, I am not a bad spirit." When we talk about bad spirits let's clarify one thing, bad means the opposite of good. In human terms, the word bad means evil. In spiritual terms the word bad means sadness. The sadness comes from a number of endeavors throughout your life, and the lives you had before. When I say sadness, understand that the soul is marked in a way where it cannot release certain energies and go on with a new life. When you hear the term, holes in the soul, or if a person announces that they carry a weight on their shoulders, and they feel this weight has been with them since birth, the reason might be they never relinquished upsetting facts on the other side. It might be something that you did not deal with regarding past lives and where you can't let it go. When this happens you bring back the sadness with you.

Sometimes bad spirits will be masked as good spirits. Why do they try to fool us? It is easier for them to attach to a human soul when they show themselves as a good spirit. If they connect to a mortal, they are in search of a life or trying to repeat a life that they did not understand. They will not hurt a mortal; they just want to be nearby in a selfish way so they can hold on to the sadness. You have all seen sadness in your life, whether in your family or just out in the world you live. The sadness you take in will grow inside of you and, with this, a soul will need to release that energy or give it away. The energy can be referred to as hot energy and needs to be handed off to another human.

Mortals release their sadness with anger. A spirit will do the same by locating a human soul that is willing to take this energy. If a sad soul will not release the sadness after a long period of time, they might turn that energy out into the atmosphere.

What is the percentage of bad spirits versus good spirits?

I would say there could be about 10 % that hold sadness and 90% good. A good spirit will work to improve and to give guidance. They will not interfere with your life, but they will become your helper. The other 10 % stay by themselves or if they join their spiritual family they might not communicate or settle in like they should. All spirits try communicating to the ones that hold sadness and give love to them, so they too can make a choice that will benefit the soul. Spirit is a human's closest connection not only to their body's soul, but also to Heaven.

The best thing to do is test each spirit that comes to you. How do you test a spirit? First you must cover yourself with white light to protect your own soul. Visualize a stream of light covering your body, if this is difficult for you to do, you can use a flashlight and hold it over your body. Once this is done, ask them if they are from the Christ light, which is a pure energy. If they cannot answer, they might carry sadness in their soul. This does not mean they will harm you, but they can steal your energy, or want to remain around you. Some will have no idea if they have a bad spirit around until they feel their energy level going down or see changes in themselves that persist for a long period of time.

What will a sad spirit look for if they want to release

this energy? They will look for a human who is willing to furnish them with energy and allow them to have their way with their mortal life. Some bad spirits will look for an opening. An opening is when a mortal is in an altered state of mind or is looking to depart. If a mortal will turn from his or her own guidance or spirit, a bad spirit might jump in. Bad spirits have a need to give off the hot energy, maybe to a person who loves greed or power. This is an opening. The one thing that you should know about bad spirits, their energy can burn out very easily because good spirits will be trying to give them love. I have been with Liz for many years. A bad spirit could not keep the energy going that long. This is the same with a human, if you are sad or down you will become tired easily. A sad spirit will try to rob you of energy so they can continue with their sadness. Most of the time they will need to move from mortal to mortal to be able to gather enough energy to exist.

Can you bring a bad spirit back with you? No, but you can bring back negativity. This can come from a past life where you still need to work on some level. An example of this would be a person who had a temper from the time they were born. The temper is from not having an understanding of a past life and returning to a mortal life before completing the lesson on the other side. Maybe through life this will ease or go away. If a soul returns with some negativity they will ask for guidance to be with them at all times. Sometimes they will come back with someone who will have the strength to teach them to let go of the temper.

Is there a Satan?

No, this is a term that mortals will refer to so they can separate in their mind acts of good versus bad. A soul will make mistakes in life. Some look at this as a sin or evil. With this they feel they need to be punished and have a Hell, opposite of spiritual world. What you need to know is that you create your own hell or Satan, not only here but also after death. When a soul crosses over and they feel they have sinned, the soul might not relax and there can be confusion. If they communicate to whomever in the rest stage that they know they have sinned and believe they should be punished for their sins, the spirits will create what will appear as Hell for them. The hell does not mean fire or chains as you would see in theaters, it does mean that the soul will be shown their sadness, or what mortals call sin, and will be given a task that will allow them to feel this sin in their soul. Many times after being put through this, the soul will relax and will be returned to the rest stage.

Let's talk about the spirits I call Ears, and the job they do.

They listen to you. They will hear your prayers when you ask out loud for help. They can pick up on the thoughts you release out to spiritual world or when you communicate to spirit. At this point they will go back and find your guide, someone who is close to you, someone who will be able to work with you. Another job they do is relay when a guide gives communication to a human from a soul that has passed. The relay will find the soul that has passed and communicate to them that a mortal wants to speak to them. This way there is a clear energy between the person that passed and the human. You could refer to them as the phone lines of spiritual world. They will never give you guidance themselves. You have your own guides that do this job. I will explain this more in another chapter.

Another type of spirit is Fairies.

What job do they do? Who are they? They work on what you would understand as make-believe or miracles; this is their job. They generally work with children and aging adults. A good example would be a child in a coma with little chance to live. The parents lose all hope and then the child suddenly awakens. The child will tell you they saw someone and energy was given to help them recover. That is the work of a fairy. Another example is an elderly person who is depressed, sick, etc, might all of a sudden take a turn for the better. That is also the work of a fairy. Your own guide can help you if you are depressed or in a coma. Fairies will search for souls in need, and many times will work with your guides.

Do they only work with health issues?

No, let's say you always had a dream to go somewhere that you could not afford. They will look for a way to complete that dream! Now they do not fulfill every dream, but they work hard trying. Think about Santa Claus for

a minute. Sometimes you just don't have the money, but
then out of the blue, you will find or win enough to complete Christmas. That is the work of a fairy. They take
care of the unbelievable; in the hope you will all learn to
trust more.

So you see a spirit possesses many positions, but no
matter what job they take on, they have a need to support
and send love to all.

GUIDES

In the last chapter I told you there were different names for spirits and one name is "Guides." What is a guide and why do we call them that?

Let's start with the name; it comes from the word guidance, meaning to help others, whether in life or death. There is always guidance. The world would not be here if there were no guides or guidance.

When I have a session with a person they always say, "Who is here for me?" A few know they are not alone, for everyone believes in something even if it is evil. The hard part is understanding who or what to believe in.

First, let's understand that spiritual guides walk among us here on Earth. Our children have guidance counselors. We have marriage counselors, psychologists, psychiatrists, and tour guides. The church will provide someone to give guidance. Let us not forget the ones who will give of themselves. If we stop to think about it, life includes a lot of guides attempting to provide direction. Sometimes we get turned around in the game of life. Some souls try so hard to win the game; they miss the spot they should be on. Help is always available, but many will never seek it. This is where our guides come in. They will assist us until we are back on track. When you go to church you pray, for you feel your prayers will be answered. Mortals need only to ask. Undoubtedly you will be heard whether in church or out of church.

Now take a look at spiritual guides. This will help us to understand more of what they do. I have been asked if only family members are guides. The answer is, "No." Someone who you don't know and have never spent time with can guide you.

How many guides will accompany you in life?

You can have one or you can have ten or more. There is no set number. Many times you select a soul or souls before you come into this life. Many of our soul mates are guides. If you decide to come back into this life, perhaps one of your soul mates will stay in spiritual world and be your guide. A spirit will be asked to take on a job. That job might be to give guidance in an area you might need. Your guide that is close to you will still guide you, but other spirits might also assist you. The soul that is doing the job will also learn from the guidance they give. We can have more than one guide at a time.

I call life a game and there are times when another person's guide will give us a helping hand. Guides will always stay in contact with you. There are times when a soul will have things it must do. Guides will be able to view the surroundings around you and help you. The question we need to ask ourselves is, "Will we ask for the help?"

You might feel that being a spiritual guide is a big job, and it is. There is a lot involved in this job. When you take a job as a guide, you are saying you will be close to a person, like a friend. A guide will help you to see the right choice without making it for you. A guide will seek ways to get you to understand why they are near you. When you are a child under the age of eight, you are able to see spirits or guides. When you become older you begin to depend on other mortals and push aside the spiritual side of life. Then it becomes more difficult to understand the guidance that is near you.

What exactly can a guide do for you? Let's take a look at a few examples.

If you were in a car and going very fast, you might sense a feeling that you should slow down, but you don't. That emotion is a guide telling you there can be danger ahead.

Can that guide help you if an accident does occur because you didn't listen?

Yes, they might pull the car into a different direction or even shield you from injury. If you were about to fall, a guide can aid by preventing you from being hurt. It was not too long ago that many guides were trying to help people live a life that wasn't materialistic, because there are more important things than money. Now many are experiencing financial problems because they did not change their attitude. Did you ever have a depressed moment and wish that your life could change? A guide will help you to make the right choices to get out of the situation.

Do guides watch everything you do?

No, this would require far too much energy. There are different levels of energy. What guides do is affix themselves to your energy and when your soul starts to encounter stress, or even a rush of intensity, they will be able to view you. This works in a way where the soul's emotional energy will send out a magnetic sensation that is picked up as a tone, or sound to you, and with this the guide can employ enough energy to aid you. There are times when a guide will be closer to you. Again, this has to do with energy levels. They will be able to stay around you more, or like myself with Liz, live with you. This will work where the soul of the mortal will give energy to the guide that is with them.

Will this tire the mortal?

No, the guide will leave for a period of time when the soul releases at night and sleeps. At this time, both the mortal and the guide will accumulate more energy. The extra energy will come from the planet. The atmosphere holds a lot of extra energy.

There are some cases where a guide will give wisdom. They will work with your mind. Some will listen to the thoughts that come to them and some will not. Let's say you have to make up your mind and resolve to do something. A guide might show you a better choice.

The soul loves to communicate, whether in life or in

spirit, and when a guide communicates to you, your soul will consume it like water. This communication is stored for future reference. What is stored can and will be used in cases where you might need information more than once. The mind is like a computer and the guide is the Rolodex where you go to seek support.

Try to enjoy quiet times. Many times when you are having a quiet period, a guide will give communication. There are times during your dreams that certain interactions will come from spirits. Hopefully, you will remember the dream. The shower is another place where guides will communicate. The water is healing and is energy.

When your spiritual guide knows you are in need of guidance, they can see out into your life. It is like looking into a very large television. Not just seeing the picture that is there, but also seeing an advance picture. Meaning, if you were at a movie theater, and you were looking at a certain scene (let's say a person is skydiving out of a plane) in spiritual world, you not only see them skydiving out of the plane, but beyond that. You would see where they are headed, and who is around them. The guide will give this to a person in thought or voice. They will not tell them they are going to land in a certain area, they will inform them that it might not be the best place to land so they can make another choice. If they do not make that choice, then the spirit will look for another way to help them.

You can have a soul adjustment. Sometimes people become deathly ill, and come down with the flu, etc. I am not

saying every time you come down with the flu you are being adjusted, but when you have illnesses, this is a perfect
time to have an adjustment. I have done a lot of adjusting
on Liz's soul. I would always tell her before I was going to
adjust her. The adjustments are to help her with enabling
the communication to flow better with me. Adjustments
are communications that gives the soul energy.

A lot of times walk-ins have to be adjusted. What happens to a guide when there is a walk-in, which is a switching of the souls?

For example, a person might undergo an operation, or
have an accident, which results in becoming unconscious.
This is when a soul change might occur. Now that the
souls have switched, what happens to that guide? While
this is going on, your guide will be communicating with
your soul. The guide will say, "We are going to go on." So
there is a swapping of souls and guides. It is sort of like
a baseball game where the pitcher is replaced and this
means the game might change.

A person with a scientific mind might find this happening hard to understand. Basically it is a transferring of
energy within a mass or body.

Scientists would roll over in their graves a hundred
times if they only knew just how scientific it was. There
is more science in spiritual world than what they can ever
find here on this Earth, or even in outer space.

In some cases where you see that an elderly person is
rambling on having a conversation, yet nobody is in the

room, they are communicating with spirit. This can also occur with anyone in the world. Some people might look at these mortals as being crazy, and yet they are not. For the communication is something that they hear, feel, or envision.

GUARDIAN ANGELS

What are guardian angels?

They are similar to a guide in many ways. A guardian angel will work with the religious area of life and spirit. They are spiritual beings, like guides that are doing their specific jobs. One is not better than the other, or more gifted. They have not gone through more plateaus or levels. But like a guide, they also will have responsibilities in an area they enjoy working in.

When we talk of guardian angels or heavenly angels, they go back as far as you can possibly remember, to the beginning of the Bible. A lot of people assume that angels have wings that carry them. What you are seeing is the energy around the angel. An angel can produce more energy than a guide. The energy of a guide will be used to help each soul they are with at that moment. Angels can work with one soul, but many times they will be with groups. You have nuns, ministers, pastors, and priests, and these are angels in a mortal aspect. People who spread religious words from a Bible are the angels of a mortal world. An angel will select this job because they will want to work with groups. They will take a large area and be able to spread their energy among all. They will work with groups that do voluntary work. Angels have the ability to gather. If the world were in need to see a change, they would take on the job of bringing souls together so that change can occur.

They also will work with groups or with a particular soul that might have problems asking for help or praying. One example is children who are living in poverty. These children will not ask for guidance. They might pray, but they wish for a miracle. They understand through their faith that angels will be worthy of answering their prayers. For angels represent GOD and the meaning of GOD.

When an angel comes, they will communicate with you in some way, and sometimes they can be seen. Remember I told you they have more energy, so it is possible to present an image. When you look into your faith, this is the core of the soul. An angel will give comfort, and over the years humans have come to realize that angels can appear and help solve their problems.

Angels will take a name. Guides will have names also, but they can change their name and many times will not reveal it. The reason an angel will hold on to a name and a guide won't is simple. The angel will perform with a large group and will need to be recognized, plus the human will need to feel that energy totally. The name gives believability and the angel will connect to that group. A guide will change his or her name if it will help you to receive the thought better. An example is a child who might take direction from a mother, before they do from a father, or vice-versa. An angel will be more willing to share of himself or herself so you will believe and have encouragement. An angel might take on a face for appearances, where a guide will work on giving the guidance through thought or sound and sometimes visual. Angels have been seen since the beginning of time. You might ask if an angel is male or female. There is no sex in spiritual world, but they will take on an appearance that gives you the most encouragement. You might have read about angels that have appeared as male or female, the sex comes from the strength of the angel. The strength is used to create a sexual tone or body.

Are there more guides than angels or the other way around?

I would say they are equal. When you take on a spiritual job, you can also change the job. You could be an angel and change to a guide, or reverse it. The freedom of choice is the beautiful part of the spiritual soul. In the game of life you also have this freedom of choice, yet people remain loyal to one choice.

How many times have you heard of a story where someone will see a statue crying, or a presence in a certain land?

This is the work of an angel. Sometimes they need to present a large display so mortals will hear their message. An angel will gather many and put them in touch with their guides. This does not mean that an angel can't or won't help them, but in general they work with large groups. It is guidance you receive from an angel, but they will put more of their energy into the request. On the other hand, a guide will seek for a better answer, or more choices for you to elect.

As mortals grow, you learn about different forms of religion, which might include angels, and GOD. All of this has an importance to your life. When a mortal understands that there is more to life than body and skin and that life begins from within, angels and GOD will give you support. When you pray, this teaches you to ask for help and not have fear or think you are alone in life. When you look at a person that has little faith or assumes they are alone, they need proof that there are angels and guides around them. An angel will watch out for them, even if they are a nonbeliever. Sometimes when death comes to a soul, the guide or angel will announce himself or herself. This is when a mortal will begin to have understanding, and will want to release any sadness they carried in life. They know someone has come for them, and they will see an angel or guide. The light of love to many represents angels.

An angel will adjust a group or area, meaning taking charge and assisting this area to achieve a better way. A guide is able to give an adjustment to an individual soul. Why would an area or a mortal need an adjustment?

There are different reasons. Maybe a person is working too much or has too much stress. An adjustment will allow them to see their life in a less stressful way. Sometimes an adjustment will occur during a soul change. This will help the body to adjust to the new soul and the emotions of that soul. A mortal soul can be adjusted for minor reasons such as rest, controlling tempers, power, and sometimes joining life as a human.

There are places in the world where there are wars, or conditions that need healing, through an adjustment. The adjustment can occur during weather conditions, disasters or even illness. If an area of the world has a lot of stress or sadness, a disaster might occur. The energy becomes so great that it has to release. When this happens it can cause weather conditions or earth changes. An angel will work to strengthen the souls in that area so they can rebuild. Angels will help each individual to move on with their lives.

When an individual is adjusted they will be given rest either through illness or sleep. It can happen during an operation, a deep sleep, and so on. With a country or a group of people, an angel will cover the area in white light and help to give that area peace. Angels might give an area a snowstorm or extreme heat. This will put people together or slow their energy down, so the soul will be able to communicate with others.

An adjustment of a soul is to take a soul back, to give the soul knowledge, and help the soul to move forward. Many times in different parts of the world when a group of souls will hold on to hatred, the angels will give a lot of energy in hope that they will accept love and that love will bring about change.

The best example I can give would be if you saw some-one who is out of control in his or her life. This can be caused by stress, greed, anger, and even bad habits. They could come down with the flu, headaches, or feel the need to sleep a lot. In most cases the adjustment does help, for the communication that spirit gives shows them doors to open. There is the possibility they will refuse it, but the offering will appear again.

Angels and the guides will come to you in your life. Be sure to ask for the help you need. When you ask, be correct in what you say, for guides and angels will help you with only what you ask for. In a mortal life, what is important to mortals, might not be important to spirit.

GHOSTS

Did you ever see a ghost?

Find ghosts to be scary?

Some do not believe in ghosts. Confused about the issue?

What is the difference between a ghost and a spirit?

Let me explain a ghost from a spirit perspective.

We talked earlier about your soul. If you remember, your soul has two separate parts, an inner soul and an outer soul. The outer part controls the body and character. The inner part controls the feelings and emotions. When we talk about ghosts, we are speaking about the outer part of the soul. So, let's understand that part. The outer soul is the connection to a ghost.

We will start from the beginning. How does a spiritual soul become a ghost? While you are passing over, the inner part of your soul will begin to lift and go with the energy that came to the soul. At the same time, the inner soul is communicating back to the outer soul "To Come," which means the outer part of the soul needs to follow, so both parts will pass together. If for some reason the outer soul decides to stay in the mortal light, then the soul will not have a complete return. The outer part of the soul might want to remain to be near a mortal. The inner soul will linger in the vision of light for a period of time, waiting for the outer part to arrive. During this time, the outer part of the soul will become perplexed with the direction it will take. The outer part of the soul will begin to release all communication with the inner part of the soul and decide to stay. With this, the inner soul will depart and go on to spiritual world. This does not mean they will not be able to communicate later after the rest stage. Now understand, the soul is two distinct parts of an energy with separate jobs. Mortals will think of themselves as one soul, so it is hard to visualize their soul in two parts.

You might ask why the inner part or the guide that is with the soul won't cross back and capture the outer part. When the soul lifts to go with spirit and is in the vision of light, the energy covers them and secures them. This will keep the soul shielded in the transformation. There is hope that the outer part of the soul will eventually realize they will not lose what is left behind and enter into the light.

Now we have a body that will deteriorate, and the outer part of the soul is still with the body not on the inside but next to the body. The outer part of your soul, as you know, works with the subconscious mind. A ghost is the subconscious, without a body or emotions. A ghost will pick up energy from surrounding mortals so it can be near a body or a place. The ghost is a spiritual soul, which is using the subconscious part of the mind and other's energies. This soul is not at peace and is confused in many ways. Understand that after death a soul that crossed can view the burial. If the outer soul remains around the body after burial there can be a chance the soul will want to reenter the body.

Now you might ask why ghosts haunt homes or buildings? A ghost that is with a body after death might see the body is deteriorating and will go back to what is familiar to them; the home or area the body lived. Many times a soul will become very close to a body or a spot in life and wants to remain with it. An example is a person who might be extremely vain, and love the body so much they might want to stay with the body. It will possibly stay at the cemetery or the former habitation. You must remember that the outer soul is relying on the subconscious, which is memories, and will return to what it knows. When the body is no longer perceptible, the soul will find a familiar material object to be with.

How far will the soul be able to travel if it leaves the body? The soul will use whatever energy it stored to return to a place it knows, for example, a house. It will wait for energy to come to it. Anyone that enters the house will give up energy to the ghost.

How does the ghost get this energy?

It pulls energy from your subconscious or from whatever is around. When it takes this energy in, it is feeding itself to survive. A pulling of energy is when a ghost will attach itself to another soul's energy. The ghost will block the mortals' energy through thought. The mortal might begin to daydream or relax into a calm state. Their energy will lift above the body and the ghost will seize the energy. This is why some ghosts will survive a long time. The mortals have no idea what is happening. The ghost will work with the person's subconscious mind almost like a spell. Most mortals love to remiss and allow the subconscious to come in. When a ghost is around they will help the mortal to do this with communicating to the mortal.

For example, a ghost leaves the body and returns to a place where it feels comfortable, perhaps their former home. With this, it will literally just move right in. In this case, it is a friendly ghost. It is very content just being in the house, and being with the person that it loved, or the person that they had shared a home with, or just being in the home itself.

What will this ghost do in this home?

It will exist.

Now, what does a ghost do in this instance? Does it walk around? Does it need to rest?

In some cases, the outer part of the soul will rest. In most instances it will basically move around the house.

Why do people see ghosts?

If a ghost pulls enough energy, it will be able to be seen by whoever is around them. The energy they will pull will allow you to have a glimpse or a feeling that they are there.

They can also move objects. This is why you hear people say "I had a chair sitting in the corner, now my chair is sitting over there. I didn't move it. How did it get over there?"

Now you have an instance where this ghost is living a life. I want you to understand it is not a happy life. When the outer part of your soul, (your subconscious) stays in a mortal existence, it is not content. The ghost will begin to imitate the mortal, and pick up mannerisms of the mortal. They will allow past lives to come in now and then, but what they really want is the old life back. If it is allowed to live in the house and no fear is shown from the mortal, the ghost could help the mortal. What I mean is a bond could be formed and the ghost will attach to the energy of the mortal where it will believe it is the mortal.

Will the ghost hurt the person that it is living with?

Not necessarily.

Can it pull so much energy from the person that it kills that person?

What it does is frighten, and sometimes it can tire that person depending on their energy level. It depends on the spirit, the soul that they hold. If they have a lower level type soul that is weaker, yes, it can really cause some damage. If they have a stronger, higher level then they will survive quite well. The person that they are with can survive and maybe not even notice them.

What image will this ghost take?

It could take on an image of their body that was just

buried or even one of a prominent past life. If someone took a picture of it, they would see a man, or a woman, whomever. Not all ghosts will show themselves. No, they are not being shy, just smart. Being seen could mean they will have to depart or be asked to cross over.

Can a ghost change sexes?

Yes.

If a ghost is in a home for twenty six years, can it go back to pick up a life that was two hundred years ago?

Yes it can, the chances are slim, about 10% chance that it would do that. If a ghost does this and permits a past energy to come in and remain for a period of time, they will have to look for comparable surroundings to match the life. Remember they stay to be with someone or a material object. A photographer with a high-powered camera might be able to take a picture of this ghost. The ghost can show the past life one day and then take on an image of another life that could be from two hundred years before. Ghosts are not camera shy. As far as they are concerned, they are still living. They exist. They know that the body is gone, but it is like telling someone who has a mental block that you shouldn't do this, and they keep right on doing it. They push everything away and do not wish to hear differently.

Now what you might be asking yourself: "What happened to the inner soul that it was connected to?" Believe me it's not a pleasant thing. Spiritual world doesn't like it.

It's like having a child who is supposed to be standing near you but instead leaves you. Now you have to go after them. It is not that simple. Number one, a lot of spirits don't even want to be around a ghost. You're supposed to have passed over. Their energies are now mixed and the energy of the ghost becomes heavy. This is because they take energy from other mortals. This energy cannot be given back to the mortals, but a guide will have to help the ghost to dispose it out into the atmosphere. When a mortal lifts to pass over, their mortal energy will begin to release. In the case of a ghost, there will be the outer soul that is the ghost, plus any energy that was pulled from another mortal's inner soul. This energy has more emotion and can cause the soul pain if it does decide to cross over.

There is a job that guides will do to retrieve a ghost. They will communicate and go into the light hoping that the lost soul will communicate back to them. The ghost has a choice. A lot of ghosts will go back. But it is very difficult because the soul is even fonder of the mortal life. Now the mortal and the ghost share a common bond in life.

Many times what keeps a ghost is mortal energy. Some people like their ghosts, they are proud of them. They brag about the things that happen to them. It's almost like having an extra person in the house, or a friend.

What a person can do to help the ghost is prayer, and asking the ghost to leave and not return. This will help the ghost to pass back over, realizing that the mortal is not holding on to them any longer. There will always be the light waiting for them. The inner part of the soul will greet and connect to complete the process.

If you want to remove a ghost, take seven white candles and line them in a straight row in front of the main door of your house. Begin to communicate with the ghost. You can say that I want you to go. You must feel this from within your soul. You start from the beginning, furthest candle from the front of the door and you start to walk backwards towards the door. As you walk backwards, you will say the Lord's Prayer, or any prayer. This could take a little time. It's not going to be an instant thing. By doing this, it will cut down on the energy of the ghost. You will be communicating to the ghost the same way the inner soul did at the time of death. The ghost will realize that you also want them to cross over and this will cause the ghost to be miserable.

Just like the subconscious mind can go crazy, a ghost can also go crazy. If a ghost does not get enough energy, it can become vicious, nasty, hateful, and start to do things.

If for some reason the ghost moves back to the house where the body lived, and someone else is living in that house, and they don't know them, this energy might not come easily. It might not be as open as a family member. A ghost might try to get rid of them. This is why a lot of times you hear people say, "We can't live in this house."

The shutters are banging, and the bed is shaking, etc. This ghost wants to come back, and have the same life it had with the body. The outer soul will hope that the inner soul will join them, even though it knows it won't, but it has hopes.

Can this ghost kill?

"Yes it could, but if it does kill, it's accidental." A ghost will try to get rid of you, and while trying to get rid of you they might move something that could fall on you or be in the way where you will trip. They have enough energy and if they work with your energy, they will be able to do this.

Will this outer part of the soul feel bad about killing you?

No, and yes. It depends on whom it kills or hurts. If the ghost wants you gone because you're not the person they came back to be with, it could. If this did happen, the ghost would be able to see the soul ascend from the person they accidentally killed. There could even be communicating between the two souls. In most cases the other soul will go toward the light and with whoever comes for them. There are cases where the soul that was killed will join the ghost. They might want understanding as to why this happened or even feel that they have a need to stay.

"Can ghosts multiply?"

Yes, if this does happen then that house or area will be dealing with a dual energy that can communicate.

Did you ever hear of a ghost town?

There are situations where a home or area will have

more than one ghost. A few things might have transpired. If a ghost is a family member and the family understands this and welcomes this, they too might become ghosts after death. The objective is so the family will stay together, or part of a family. If a ghost is in an area and there is another ghost in that same area they can pair up. A ghost will need energy to survive and the more the merrier.

So many perceive that ghosts are here to haunt and give fear, not true. A ghost wants peace. It might sense that what is on the Earth plane will give them that peace and withdrawing from it will leave them unsettled.

Will a ghost ever leave the location? Some might move on if they begin to understand that the area does not pertain to them any longer. The energy will seek another place to stay and will become weak. It might acquire energy, but the energy will not fulfill the ghost. This could be a time when the spirit can call to them, and the soul will depart.

Can you touch a ghost?

How would it feel?

You wouldn't feel anything, as far as feeling skin or substance; however, you might feel energy. You might feel the same if a spirit was with you. Feel a cool air that goes past you. What you can feel just depends on the energy. If you feel a touch from a ghost, this is an energy that the ghost will relate to your brain. The energy will give your brain a picture of the touch. This picture can transform into feeling, and from that point you have an understanding that another is with you.

Will a ghost ever help a mortal in life?

They have the ability to guide as well as a spirit if they wish to. If a ghost is with you in your home, they might become attached to you even if you are not their family. They might befriend you, and with this they will assist you in that area. They could travel with you if the energy is there, but most will stay where it is comfortable and familiar. There can be time when they will give you things they think you need. Many want you to like them so they can remain. They look at things differently for they feel that peace can come to them in the mortal life, and they see themselves as a body. They will use your energy and brainpower in various ways to accomplish things.

It is best for a ghost to return to spiritual world. The energy they carry will be restored, and they can return if they choose. A ghost is a soul that is only a cover for the emotion and thought that has passed on. Like a cover of a book, if it's not restored it will begin to fade and deteriorate. If you have a ghost around you, tell them they must cross over, give them prayer, and reassure them that they will feel at peace and be given guidance.

WHERE IS SPIRITUAL WORLD?

I have been asked the question. "Where is spiritual world?"

The best answer I can give is, it is past the sun. If you were able to go into the sun and pass through to the other side, you would have a clearer view of what I am about to explain. It is a totally different atmosphere. If I had to describe it to you, I would use the words flat, cool, damp, and dim. The coolness meaning a mortal would feel colder there carrying the skin that covers them. The surroundings are dim not as bright as Earth. When I say damp I mean like a fresh morning dew. This is not another planet, it is another world. You might ask why the conditions are different and I refer to this as another world. The conditions I refer to help the soul to stay strong and healthy. The water factor is a healing tool. Here on Earth, water is also used to heal and cleanse. The soul does not have skin or outer covering, as the mortal does. Here the human skin will protect your soul from different elements the atmosphere has. As for the dimness, after you pass there is no need for eyes, the soul can see through communication. The dimness also will assist the soul in viewing out to different worlds.

I'm going to start with death. It's a word most of you fear and have little understanding of.

Where do we go when we pass over? Some people feel we don't go anywhere. They are right in many ways. Because they know that this life is an individual life; that this life is something that they live and once it's over, it's over. They feel that life is only when you have skin and you are on Earth. I have heard many discuss living, and they feel their soul will rise, but they feel the soul is part of death, not the living. I hope to give you insight so you understand that the soul is life here on Earth and also when you pass. In spiritual life you will not remember as you do here on Earth. Why is this? Well, in spirit there is no need to store. The reason is communication. It is free. When you communicate in spirit you share, and then it is released. Can you think back on a time when you felt the openness of communication, and afterward you let it go?

However, the soul will continue on, and with this a new life will start in spiritual world. Have you ever heard people say that they see a light come to them? This is a comforting light that makes them feel good when the time of death does come. It will help them to cross over. This is referred to as spiritual light. I know you have heard others say they have seen this light during near death experiences. There can be times when the soul will come close to death, but there is no light. This is a time when communication will take place, to agree on something, or to give an adjustment to the human. This is something that took place when I came to Liz and asked if she would work with me. There was no light only communication and adjusting. This can also occur when a soul is switched, as in Liz's case.

Now let's look at a situation where a person will suddenly die. Many will ask if there is a light? When a sudden death occurs, the soul's guide will lift them from the body in fractions of seconds before it happens. Let's say an accident or a terrorizing act happens to a person. The person will not feel the afflicting pain.

There are times when I will inform a person to put spiritual light around themselves and others. This is a form of protection for the human soul. The question has been asked as why some who had a near death experience have never seen the light, yet others do? The reason for this is the spirit that will come to them can block the light, the doorway. The light is very bright, and it can take on an image of a tunnel. It's not a tunnel. It's a stream of love or energy that will surround your soul, and stem out into a direction so the soul will be guided. This light is cool and damp. This will help preserve the soul, since the body is no longer attached to give it protection. The journey in which your soul will cross over varies in time. This is why for some it is not that long of a journey. Some will be so happy to be joined by loved ones that they will not realize the journey.

Many I have spoken to fear death. Not only the crossing, but also the place they will go. Let's start with what has been joked about or said in jest. "The Pearly Gates" or "Saint Peter." Well, some of this is true. There are no gates. As for "Saint Peter," there are many souls to greet you. They are other souls that were close to you or might have communicated with you, either in the mortal or spiritual. This can be one soul or a group of souls. They will give you communication as to where you are and help you become settled in spiritual world. They will scan your soul to see how you are adjusting. The reason for this is that many will feel that they should not be there or some might feel they have reached this world before their time. They might feel that they should be someplace else. Possibly hell, "I'm supposed to go in the other direction." With this, spirits can assist them to relax, and take them to a resting place.

In some cases Spirit must display a form of hell to relax the soul. So you see that death for some is what you have an opinion of. It is not to fear. Sometimes the opinion you carry through life will surround you in death. If you were frightened at an early age, this could even last after crossing over. If you were given a direct rule to carry with you in life, a belief, or even a fairy tale this can be carried over. Some feel that if you slip up in life and sin, those sins will be punished. There is no punishment in spiritual world. What you refer to as a sin, this is an energy that was not needed in your mortal time. You store this energy hoping you will be forgiven. When you pass over, this energy will be cleansed the same way as the energy stress. It will be taken from your soul, and released out of spiritual world. If you need to have understanding of your life and your sins, or what you think of as sins, this will be given to you in the rest stage. As to the question of karma, this is a choice. It is not something that has to be done. Sins, if you want to use that word, are choices in your life that were not supposed to occur. This becomes a part of you, and you need to allow the soul to breathe after death. So spirit can assist you with this.

When you close your eyes at night and go to sleep this is like dying. Death is just a matter of slipping from one existence to another. It is very beautiful and relaxing.

Did you ever listen to classical music and feel your whole body relax? Classical music is connected with spiritual world. It is a music that started years ago and has been given to us to help us unravel from the human occurrence. For some that might have a near death experience, they might hear a tone or sound. This sound is similar to classical music. It will relax the soul, and the tone will give a direction also.

Let's discuss what your soul will feel like in the light of energy that will carry you from one existence to another. I will give you a few explanations. Think about smoke. The way smoke moves could be used as one way. A slow moving cloud of smoke will take a shape and move upward until it disappears. Another way is if you were in a body of water, and someone told you to relax and go limp and float. The body will be still, but the soul will release its energy and float above. Will you feel like yourself? Yes, but without the body. The heaviness will become light, but the form and thought will be light as in a dream state. The soul feels no pain. There is no hurt. There is no memory. There is no guilt. It is as if you have taken your body and cleansed it. So if you have a fear of death, I would say you are wasting energy.

When you decide to leave the human world and go to the spiritual one, it is your soul's choice. So why make that choice if you like where you are? Some will have communication from a soul in spiritual world asking them to return. Others might connect with spirit while in a dream and decide they want to return. There could be a case where a person is ill and while on medicine their soul will release above them and spirit will communicate to them. They could be near death and a mortal might appear to them as a person that had passed and they will let go and want to follow spirit. Some will recall a choice that was made before they came to the mortal world and follow through with that choice. Some ask to return for peace.

Even in the case of a severe accident, fires, etc, there is always someone there to help the soul adjust, so you are never alone. When I speak of choice, you will always have a choice here on the Earth plane and in spirit world.

The question has been asked, "When does the soul make the choice to die?" "If there is an accident, how could the soul make a choice like this?"

The choice is made at many different times, before life, during life, and even in the womb itself. There are some accidents in life where you did not make a choice. With this, you will be able to return and be given back that life in some form. Even in spirit there are some accidents that are truly an accident.

You will not be in a place where you are frightened or scared. Think about a dream possibly that you have had in your lifetime where everything is beautiful. You awake with comfort, plus you will feel rested. When you cross you will feel the same way. You will begin to feel the difference promptly after death.

So now, I hope you have an understanding as to what you will feel when you arrive? Let's discuss what will happen, although, I must tell you it does vary for some. The first thing is that you will not see things like you do here in this world. You will communicate with emotions and thoughts. A blind person will understand this part. You must remember there is no body or eyes to attend to. The atmosphere is different. Much dimmer than the world you left. This does not mean you will be in darkness. If you had eyes it might seem dim, but for spirit it is not. The thoughts and the emotions will bring beauty to it. You will see that communication is a big word. Why? Because the soul will need to express as it does here. In the human world you hold back your emotions and some thoughts. In spiritual world it is automatic. The first step is to rest. You will be taken to a rest place where you will be joined by other souls that you are familiar with. Here you will be able to receive more understanding of your surroundings. This rest place is where you will view what you stored in your soul and the subconscious mind. The time period here can also vary depending on how the soul will accept the transformation. While you are in the rest spot, you will receive communication about what is around you. This is like a diagram, but it will be given through a thought process. The communication will be given not only by souls that are close to you, but also by selected workers that have this job.

Are you wondering if there is work after death?

Well, there is. At this time you will be allowed to adjust major issues that you might have had while on Earth. So you see, you will have a time to rest and to communicate about what you might not understand. The period of time you will remain here is up to your individual soul. There are some souls that will remain here a very short time. Some have more understanding, and some want to move on with things. With each soul it differs as it does here in a human form. After the rest stage is over, you and loved ones will be able to be together as a spiritual family or you might go off on your own.

Spiritual world is like this world. A soul will have a job and a family. After you crossover and have completed the rest stage, then you will be able to pick a job. You will also be asked if you would like to reincarnate. So you see spirits are much like you.

You might ask me why a soul will be alone in spiritual world, if this is a place of love?

The answer to that is, choice. Each soul has a choice, and some wish to venture out on their own. This does not mean they will not connect at some point in time with other souls. As life is a game and fun, spirit is an adventure that can reoccur and change often. While you are with loved ones or souls from the past, you might take a job. If you take a job you might be asked to teach, give guidance, or even be ears, which is a link to the human requests. You will work closely with other spirits communicating with life, and with the ones that are with you in spiritual world. Yes, even there you will still learn, refresh your soul, and work out things that you brought back with you. It can be a time also to choose and select a new human life if you wish. I have been asked if you take a mate as you do here in human life. The answer is, "Yes, if you wish."

It is a time when you might rejoin with your soul mates and catch up and continue on with other souls that you have been apart from. Why not stay in spiritual world and never return? Well, there could be someone that you are very attached to on Earth, and you have a desire to return in hopes to be closer. Or maybe you feel you want the game again. But this time with more flair. Some souls will return to the game for it can be fun. Let's say the best word would be experience. If one of your soul mates were on Earth you might feel a need to be closer. Try to think about the words "starting over." How many times have you thought about starting over? When you pass, this is a clear choice for some. When you start over in spirit, you make sure you will have all the right tools this time, as you did before. This time you will play better. This is a human way to look at it. In spirit you will use the term eternal. Meaning you will never allow yourself to be stopped. That you can go on and with each time you will learn more and teach more. The return is like starring in your favorite play. You pick the characters and the theme. If you like the play it will become your soul's new life and returning. So you see whether it is here or there it is a choice, and it is fun. There will be love with a lot of understanding. You will never be alone, and you will always have the help you need. Spiritual world is like going across a creek. When you reach the other side you can look back and see all you left, and in time cross-back over. Like the example I used before with the creek, just take one step at a time, the placement of the rocks will lead you across and help you not to fall. It's a child's adventure from one world to another. Breathe and enjoy it.

A VIEW OF SPIRITUAL WORLD

So many have asked me to ask Ruthie what it looks like in spiritual world. We have all seen pictures, whether on television or in the movies, where heaven has beautiful flowers, and clouds or maybe all is snow white. This is a picture that we carry in our minds so we will be at ease, and know that we will go to a place of peace and comfort. Well, there is peace and comfort, but according to Ruthie it doesn't look like the movie.

The place she refers to as spiritual world or what you would call heaven is a plateau that is cool, damp, and dim as we said before. It will have an appearance of being flat, instead of mountains or rolling hills. Try to picture in your mind an open area, like a long road with miles of ground. The ground is not a ground like you would see on Earth. It is similar to the ground floor of an ocean without the water. The area is very large and spacious and it does have a beauty to it. The air is sweet, not a candy-coated sweet where you will think you are in a candy shop, but fresh and luscious smelling. You will be able to see out and across easily, no matter where you will be. The dampness is not felt the way you would feel it here on Earth. The souls adjust very well to the dampness, the way you would adjust to a swim in the ocean. As for being dim, you will not notice this for the soul does not have eyes. You will be able to sense and detect where you are going. The coolness is like being refreshed, as if you were outside on a pretty spring day. There are sections that go around spiritual world. They are flat in shape, dark in color. They could represent mountains to a mortal. An example of a color and a substance would be like slate. This area is used to store the unwanted energy from a soul. As a soul you will look at this as being normal, the way you look at the world you're in now.

Now you might ask where are the clouds and the flowers? Try to imagine. They are there, but you need to create them through an energy, and once they are constructed many times you will keep them. This is a picture you wish to live in. The way you create them is simple. Can you visualize a large movie screen before the picture comes on, and you create whatever you want to surround you? Now this might sound like something out of a science fiction movie, but it is not. The energy you hold in your soul will be able to generate out and formulate a spiritual life as you wish. This does not mean that spiritual world is very plain. It does mean that if you think of it as a place that is a paradise you could be displeased. Spiritual world is like a chip in a computer. It carries what a soul will yearn for and will create it for you.

The beauty is what you create plus what you can see. When you cross over you will be with someone you know and love. This in itself is a beauty to the soul and a feeling of peace. When you arrive you will be able to create what you want your spiritual life to be like, as well as the surrounding area. Let me put it another way. Let's say you will have all the tools (and I use this word as an example) to build a paradise. For some, Earth is a paradise, and some view it as a hell. It will be the same with the spiritual world you create. The energy that you bring and whoever will be around you can create a place of beauty or just an ordinary one.

When you arrive you will be greeted and recorded. In spiritual world, there are records of past lives and a place that will store past thoughts. There are souls that will be in charge of the records. Now you might ask if there is paper in spiritual world?

No, what is recorded is energy, and each part of the energy that you bring with you holds thought, memories, emotions, and characteristics. This energy is segregated into groups until you use it again.

The way it is recorded is in segments of vibrations and also tone. The brain energy is given to the Hall of Records. There a soul will be able to communicate with this energy. The keepers of the records will separate this energy of tone and mark it with a code that symbolizes your soul and past lives. If you see this tone in a mortal atmosphere, it would show as a color. Each color represents a communication. An example is like shorthand, what is recorded is important. What is not important is unwanted energy that is sent out to the "Mountains of Spirit." The mountains of spirit are located on the outer rim of spiritual world and will contain energy that is deteriorated in some way. An example would be like a virus on a computer.

The atmosphere in spiritual world is an active one. As I said before, the area is large like a country fair. Like a day at the fair you are able to visit, select, and enjoy, and create an adventure. The day would be full, yet you would not feel tired, for you are at peace.

When a soul arrives on the other side they might require special attention. An example would be if a person had a lifetime of drug abuse, which controlled their whole life. Their energy would be low, and the soul would need to be healed. With this an adjustment is given, where another soul or souls will instill energy and take them back to a higher level of energy. This does not mean every soul involved with drugs or other substances will need tweaking, yet there are some that can't release certain energies and need extra attention.

I spoke of energy you obtain from other souls. This energy is a natural energy, the word natural means pure, and free. When you are on earth the energy you carry in your body and soul is controlled. A mortal needs to control the energy here because of two things, area, and the body that houses the soul. The area here is a smaller area where a spiritual energy has a difficult time releasing. The bodies that house the soul's energy hold back that energy and keep it intact. When you hear the saying, "You are more." this is true. The mortal body and soul will store a certain amount of energy. This energy can come through at certain times, but the body keeps it intact until the soul returns to spiritual world. The energy that I'm referring to is when you can lift a car or go for days without food, in cases of emergency, etc. This is when the soul will pull from their reserves and give to the body. Your guide can also supply you with energy in case of an emergency. The soul knows this and will use less of the energy. If this energy were to be released by humans, planet Earth would not be able to hold all of it and with this, many things could happen. The ocean could become forceful. There could be a lot of natural weather, and mind changes. When the soul is released from the body and crosses over, this energy is more relaxed and has more room to expand. This is why a spiritual soul can communicate out to mortals or wherever. A mortal might not understand, yet know that it is possible to communicate out to loved ones who have crossed, but are not sure how to do it.

So if you were wondering if you could move buildings or overpower a person with your mind, I would say it is possible. Every spiritual soul will carry a certain amount of energy. Some might have more, some less. How can you tell here on Earth who has the most?

You might not be able to. If you feel the powerful have more, you are wrong. It doesn't have to do with size or intelligence. The smallest person and one with little thought could have more energy. So what is the purpose of more energy versus less energy?

Nothing, again it is a choice. I know you must be sick of hearing the word choice, but it is a word that mortals need to understand. If mortals have more understanding of choice, the world would be able to come together and enjoy peace and love. No mortal would feel they must die to have total peace, and there wouldn't be a desire to have more. When you are in spiritual world, your desires are put to use. You will not spend endless energy trying to win or to beat someone. You will be able to communicate and create with other souls. Now you might ask "Why can't I create here?"

You can on a smaller level, and some do. Most will put their energy into wasteful hours of trying to become something they won't enjoy. When you are in spirit, you begin to relax, and your energy will totally release. It's like letting out a scream. You feel relief. Your energizer will move about, and you will begin to create.

I told you that you will create a picture or existence, and you will keep it. You will be able to change this if you wish. Yes, again choice. When your energy mixes with a loved one's energies you will become peaceful, and you will feel enjoyment. I know what you are thinking. What if your loved ones are there, and you are here? First thing you must remember you can always communicate to whomever, even if they have passed over to spiritual world. You must allow your energy to go out and to cross over. This does not mean you will die, but you need to feel you are with them. If you close the door and say to yourself, I have lost them, you are telling them you do not want to communicate. They will wait, if that is their choice. If you open the door of life and death so that communication is the link between you both, then you will have peace and know enjoyment.

A life in spirit can be like a life you have here on Earth, only without skin. The importance of skin is to harbor the soul and to be seen. A mortal person cannot sense the soul of another, as it would in spirit, so the skin is the mass that is created so less energy will be used. Since you will be working with a lower energy, the skin becomes your identity. A mortal will depend on their body for just about everything. A spirit will depend on their inner energy.

If someone close to you crosses over, the remaining souls will focus on the passing of the body. Try focusing on the energy the person had. Start with the love you felt. Remember the feeling they gave you. Look around a room and think about their thoughts. While they were with you, did you ever see them stare and wonder what they were thinking? At that point in time you might have focused in on their thoughts. This is the same thing. If a person closes their eyes and let their souls take charge, they will be able to communicate with another person. This also holds true with spirit. In spiritual world you will communicate with many if you choose, and you will view the soul and the energies.

While in spiritual world, you will connect with souls that you know and have been involved with in some way. Many times you will stay together as a family. There are clusters of souls that stay together for some time. They will interact with each other and often work with each other. The families that are close will build their energies and can create a home. Now you might not have a house and yard like you do here, but you will have a feeling like you do. When a family is created they will do this through thought. They will select what they enjoyed in their mortal life or even in a spiritual life. A soul will not need to be protected from weather elements so there are no material objects in spiritual world. You might ask questions like, "Do you sleep, eat, dress, and socialize?"

The answer is "Yes, you can." You will have to do so through a sensation and focusing out your thoughts. The thoughts are what you took in and put into your subconscious. So you see your memories of each life can be very valuable to you when in spirit. I told you that life is like a game. While in spiritual world, you want to remember the enjoyment of the game. So you will go back into your thoughts of a prominent life or one that you enjoyed, and you will take from it. You might start with something you will recall that appealed to you. From there you will continue on, and begin to build what you need and want in your spiritual life. When you focus on this it will begin to materialize, and you will start to sense it around you. For some they will focus on the flowers and beautiful things, the way they believe it should be.

As souls settle in they will search for (if not already with) other souls that they consider family or close friends. With this they will build their spiritual home, and continue on. They will select a job to do, and some will even go to different elevations to learn or to teach. To give you a little more on the creation of the spiritual life, let's take it in steps.

The first step is to come from the rest place and settle with whomever you may choose.

The next step is to communicate out to the souls that are around you, and even to ones that are still on a mortal plane. Some souls might want to stay connected to a mortal, and do less communicating to spirit. If the soul decides on this, this is fine. At this time they will select a job to do, and that job could be to be near a loved one that they left. Now you will ask if that soul will create a home or place in spirit?

Well, if a soul wishes to be near a mortal they might house themselves in the mortal home. That is why some might feel spirit near them more than others. As in the case with Liz and myself, I stay in her home. This is my family now. The next step for some will be to gather with loved ones or friends with whom they shared a former life. After the communication these souls will begin to put their energies together. When they do this they will all contribute a little from a past life or something that is needed.

The energy will come together and begin to build a foundation, or area, where those energies can stay and communicate. In some ways the energy would remind you of a bee's nest. All the energy will be working and feeding off of each other. The souls that will be present will be able to view the situation, and if they had eyes would see a home and surroundings.

In the next step each soul will select a job to do. As you learned before, it could be a guide, angel, fairy, or even a soul that will instruct in spiritual world. There are jobs that are associated with other jobs.

So now you have a spiritual creation, where the soul can live in spiritual world as long as they wish. If they wish to reincarnate they can do this also.

Is the world of spirit a beautiful place?

Yes, there is peace and love, and family that will give enjoyment. The soul will be able to breathe. There is no competition to win, only an openness to communicate and express. With this you have peace in your soul, and when you return you will bring that peace back with you.

PICKING

When a soul wants to come back to a life here on Earth, they will find a soul to come with, or will come back to a soul that has already arrived. They must pick a life, and the basics that they will need to have in that life. I will give you an idea of how they go about doing this. Let's start with the soul's decision to return. This will come to a soul either through an agreement or a view. The view is when a spirit will see a soul on the Earth plane; they will select a person near that soul that is about to die or who is willing to switch souls. When there is a soul switching this is called a walk-in. If they decide to take on a new life, they can still be near that person on earth. They might come back as a relative, neighbor, or even a friend's child. The decision is made, and with this they must prepare to return. At this point this soul will need to pick a life that will suit them in mortal world. When I speak of your spot in life, this is what a soul will select. I will give you understanding of what is selected for your spot. See if you can visualize this. I think it will help.

You will need protection in a mortal life, whether it is

from other mortals or elements. With this, you will choose
a strength, and endurance. The next is style. You will pick
an appearance, not only of body, but inner soul, which is
your character. You will pick capability, and this is talent,
and knowledge. You will also choose your constitution,
which is the health of the body and the mind. These energies are placed in the core of the soul and will stay with
the soul throughout life. Your spot or core of the soul will
contain the basics you need in life, so you will be able to
start and build on your life. This energy will show to some
as a color. All the energy blends together, and this will
project as a color which some call your aura.

At this time, you will choose a place that will be near
or with the other soul. Now if you have an agreement
with a soul while in spiritual word, you both will select
an adventure. The adventure can consist of many things,
you might select a place where you will meet and become
mates, even enemies. You can return as twins, or friends,
or even relatives. An example could be babies born around
the same time in a family. If a soul wants to return to a
soul in a mortal life, they could come back as relative,
even animal. Many times souls will stay with their spiritual families even here on Earth plane. At this stage you
need to scan an area to live. If the person is on the Earth
plane or even on another planet you will then prepare your
life to settle with their life. The return can also involve a
group of souls. The group can be from one spiritual fam-

ily or souls that just want to return and be in the same area.

Next you must choose what you would like to do or the adventure you would like to have. The reason for the word adventure is to let you know that life is fun, and you need understanding and to love it.

When we look at life on this plane, you have many things that you will come into contact with throughout your life.

We have fear, love, hate, jealously, luck, being unlucky, etc. This is where the basics you select for your spot will come in handy, because the basics can manage some of this.

You might choose to return to a soul that is experiencing fear. You might return not only to be with them, but also to aid them with the fear factor. The strength you selected might also be able to see them through. Now if the mortal is an adult and the soul that will come is an infant, you might ask, "How is this done?"

Even though a baby, a child can help an adult soul by giving comfort, leading them to other areas in their life, keeping them alert. You might want or they might just want you to be with them. You might have to deal with fear or other factors, and with this you will be able to pull from your spot the basics you need to assist in this life. So you see, many times you have more help than you know.

Now the basic life is set. You have the basics down, now you choose the extras. With this, you will want to build on what I call your border in your soul. The way you will do this is you will review the past lives you were in. You will then pick a prominent ability or even a life that you want to take from. This means you can select different personalities for different parts of your life. As the life goes on, you will need borders for certain parts of that life. The borders will line the energy of the mind. If the mind cannot find a solution or guidance, it will pull from the border. This is the subconscious mind. At various times a soul will revert back to a past life for support. This can occur during stress or illness.

Let's talk about understanding, this is the ability to look at life or whatever and see the total picture. Understanding will take you to a point where you can make decisions in your life, and from that you will learn right and wrong. If you have problems with understanding, you can pull from the subconscious mind. The subconscious will find a life that can supply those energies to your soul. Your guide can also assist you in this area; they can perform an adjustment or send you help.

The body becomes a creation of all the energy that a soul will pull together for this life. The soul has a soft side, and a side that is strong. When you come into life you bring both the male and the female energy with you. You might choose a stronger energy to be the dominant energy, meaning you will be a male, or in reverse a softer energy, meaning you will become a female. Sometimes you might not choose a strength completely until you reach the age of eight when spirit leaves you. If the soul didn't select a path, then they might be unsure of the energy they will need to complete the game. They might select a person to be with, but didn't decide whether they will need a strong energy or soft. Most gay people choose their life before they come to Earth. They will select an equal amount of both, the strong versus the soft energy to help their path. An example is a soul that will choose a male body in strength, but they will pick softer emotions, the person on the Earth's plane might represent their mother in this life, where in spirit it was their mate. They will come to be opposite them as a man, yet their emotions will be soft, this will keep them from wanting them as a mate. Being a man with a softer emotion, they will look for a soul that will have understanding of their strengths and this could be another man with an equal balance of energy. If they find a female they might find it hard to love that female completely. A woman might select comparable energies as the man, only in reverse. The body being female might come to this life to live like a female, but they might need a strong emotional strength for protection, or even love. This does not mean that every man that loves their mother a lot or a woman that is strong is gay; these are only examples. If the area you select to live has little to offer, you might pick the strong side of your soul to be more in charge of the body. This way you can help yourself more. In some cases if the person is a male in this life that is waiting for you to join him, he might have asked you to be on the soft side so he can care for you. As a result, you will pick female or soft. If you wish to have a life or choose a life that would encounter hard work, you would gather all you need to help you to be strong. If you have an agreement with a soul or souls to love, teach and give, you might choose more of the softer side. Some will work both the strong and the soft parts of the soul. What this means is that they, like in spirit, see no difference between the mortal life and spirit life. Now you can begin to see your life like a blue print.

Let's look at the intellectual part of your life. You will need to select a certain amount of intelligence for a particular life. The life you select will have a lot to do with how much intelligence you give yourself, an example, you might select a life that has limits on education, so you will choose from that. This does not mean you won't have the knowledge or won't be able to advance. This means you will prepare for this lifestyle. You can always add to your intelligence. I'm sure most of you are thinking, "What about the person who lives in the worst area, with very little chance to become educated, and still does?"

I'm not saying you will choose an education according to the area you choose, but you might have to select what can be handled at that point in time. If you come to be with someone to help them in their life, you might not need to become the scholar, or pursue a degree. Even if you select a life where intelligence is not the important factor, you can also add to your intelligence at any time. There are some that select more intelligence and never use it, this is their choice. Maybe they jumped spots, or decided that they want to wait and use the knowledge at a later time. This is because it might not be needed, but will always be with you in the borders. When you return to life as a child, you select many things in the core of the soul, but you also have the free will to add or change whatever.

Lets look at the why, some point in life's game you will ask yourself why. You might not have understanding of the path you chose. This will happen to every soul, reason being that as you continue on with life you separate from the spiritual side of your life. This does not mean you have become a bad person, it means that you like others in life put your energizers into the mortal path. Let's look at the spiritual side of your soul. This is the doorway between life and spirit. The spiritual side is not religion; it is not only for the good. The spiritual part of the soul will be in each life. With this you select a partner to give you guidance. You can choose an energy that will help you to communicate back to spiritual world and to other mortals. The spiritual will give you the center eye, so you can view another's soul and see beyond life. The spiritual energy you carry will help the soul to relax and release during dreams and sex. This energy will help you to find peace in your mind and the soul.

There might be a choice to have what humans call common sense, where the mind is not the main factor, and you use more thought and visual. If you choose this you will have more energy in the body. The thought will come from

the subconscious mind. Along with this you will choose
a voice, not only in sound, but in the way you will come
across to others. The sound is the communication the
soul will throw off. This will mean in strength, ability, and
factual. The basics you select will show if you plan on being shy, outgoing, practical minded, or if you will wait for
things or you make them happen. There are many little
things that can go with all of this.

Let's look at what type of guidance you will need in this
life. Some come with little guidance. Some need more guidance all the time. This will give you the word "What?"

It will show your level of independence or dependence
upon others around you. This will also help you to select
a religion, a social group, how many friends you plan to
ask to come with you, and how many people you would
like to put in your life. This means mates, friends, family,
and how many years you need to be with all. This is also
true of animals in a human's life. Did you ever wonder
why some people have many friends and family and others
have fewer?

You selected this. Many come back with the same family or what I will call cluster of souls that have formed and
have been together in many lifetimes. You will never be
told to come back with that family, but many choose to. A
soul mate is when you spend time with another throughout many years, whether on the Earth plane or spiritual
plane or other planes in the universe.

So where does a soul collect the energy for a life? Is

there a special area where energy is stored? Yes, they are called "Plateaus." While in spiritual world you will travel to different plateaus and you will compile and store the energy for future lives.

Now if a person passes and they feel that the person or persons they left needs comfort, they might ask a soul in spiritual world to go to them in a body to represent them. A child could come into your family unexpectedly; this could be a soul that will bring life back to a family or a person. The soul might portray a style of the life that passed. The soul that will come will be in contact with the soul that passed over and will stand in for them, until the family has comfort and goes on. At the time the soul will continue on, but will work with its own energy.

When you pick things for your soul, you will be picking for yourself and also others that will surround you in that life. This doesn't mean you can not add or take away from a life, only that you bring what you need to enjoy the life and to help yourself and others. So many never use all that is on their spot, for they forget the spot and take another path. The life you picked is to share with whomever you came to. When you live a full life and use all you bring with you, this will give you happiness. Each life will add on to the eternal life, and that energy can and will be used in future lives. Take a moment and look past the skin and into the core of your life, and use all that you have brought with you, so happiness can and will be yours.

THE GAME

The game is the way I explain life. Each person comes with a spot, and on his or her spot they will have the basics to help with life.

It is an emotion that you begin to feel as a child, and it grows with you. A small child will understand their spot the moment they are born, they know that spirit is around them. Plus they have a clear understanding of their emotions. When a child becomes nine or older they will begin to see others and the spots they stand on. Some will surrender their spot because they feel another spot is better. Your spot will hold emotions, strengths, and knowledge. In order to give more detail on the word spot and to help you understand, visualize a play. Each character has their own spot they need to stand on. The part you would play starts at a certain part of the stage. It will also have a certain amount of emotion, strength, and knowledge in order for you to play the part. Everything you say and your actions begin with that spot. A spot is a starting point and an ending point in your life. I hope this will help you to understand how important your spot is. Just like a play, if you change characters or your spot, you will be another actor. The game for humans is to have fun.

You do not need to figure out life or achieve 100% in all you do. So many humans spend a good portion of their life trying to get ahead, and hope they can beat someone or have more than the neighbors or even family members. They waste a lot energy and usually never win completely anyway.

Humans can't see their energy so they can't understand or know that they are losing it.

As a child you will come to life to be with others; for example parents, friends, or even a town. The child will have a spiritual guide with them at all times. The spirit will communicate and is seen by the child. After the age of eight or nine, it differs for some; the spirit around the child is no longer visible, even though the spirit will stay near the child. The child will go on to rely on the parents or their guardians. This is when the game really begins. The child will follow, plus they will believe in what they are told or see or hear. As a child from infancy to the age of eight, you rely on all your senses and the spirit around you. This is why many children talk out loud to themselves. In fact, spirit is near them listening. A spirit will play with the child, and communicate what a parent is trying to teach the child. The earth has a lot to see, and has adventure, and when spirit releases the child, the child will rely on their eyes and ears more than other senses and spirit. The child will learn to lean on the parent or protector, as they would spirit.

As I said before, you are here to play a game. If you would use your inner self, and allow the soul to take charge, then the game would not be a struggle, as it is for many. You would enjoy life more, for you would be doing what you came for. How do you do this? First be you, your spot, second have no fear of life, for it is a game, and third use all your senses, for they will lead you.

At this time we should set the players. You will have those who will excel at everything they do. There will be others who will have to work a little harder at things. Some will come with more. Some will not care if they play or not. Some will only play to win.

There is also more than one game. This will offer you a choice, and you can switch games and players. Everyone who comes to life on Earth is here to love, have understanding of all, and to have fun. As a child you do this. As an adult you begin to feel you have to win, and you have a main reason for being here.

You might ask "What types of games are there?" It is hard to say exactly. Each person who comes will create a game. Some games are alike in some ways. You decide to return to be with other souls. In some cases you play the game with that person, and when the game ends, you might go on to another player. Some people will play a game of being alone. This might be by choice after you come; then again some choose it as part of their spot.

You will always be attached to the spiritual world, where you originally came from. This comes with you, on the spot you carry. When a soul becomes interested in the next person's spot you might begin to lose the meaning of your own. There are cases where people never enjoy what they have brought back with them. They put so much energy into getting ahead, or collecting energy from other spots, that their life becomes like a one-way street and they are going the wrong way.

Let's look at the game itself. Some humans will hold similar characteristics, or even looks, and emotions. Each human soul will be an individual, but since we are all from spirit, many will come from the same spiritual family, where there are similarities.

The game is to enjoy all that the Earth plane has to offer. This means traveling, the ability to use talent, to be able to use the mind, your feelings. There are so many possibilities, and from each of the ones I mentioned there are other links. You will never be able to do it all, and this is why you will have certain things on your spot to help you in your game.

Did you ever look back on your life and feel like you have had maybe two or even three different lives in one? These are the different games. If I could help most humans to forget the word "100%" or the word "better," and go with what they feel from within, then they would have fun. The word that so many follow and create around them is society. I call it society's handbook. I have never seen a child born with a handbook, but somewhere in their life they are supplied one and follow it.

I know you must be thinking that there are rules you need to follow in life. Well, you are right! The rules of a game will have do's and don'ts. When you look at the rules of life, there are also the do's and the don'ts; they are called the Ten Commandments. These rules were presented in the beginning of time. The reason for the rules in life is to have order, the same as with any game. Many will say that we need to have society's handbook with us at all times. This is not so. What is bestowed to all souls are basic rules. This is something you bring with you. In spiritual world you review or even learn more about honesty, loyalty, faith, charity, character, happiness, and most importantly love. All of this is in the Ten Commandments. These rules are reviewed in the church, and in all faiths. We use each of these in everyday life. So the rules are important, for they help the game to be fair and to be fun. The societal part of life is what humans have added to the rules, why I'm not sure. If you would ask me how I feel the society's handbook started, I would say the word "karma." The word means fate or necessity. So many human souls that are here play the game of life and will sometimes overlook the rules, to obtain the necessities they want. This will lead them into many different paths and will help them to jump spots.

The soul will hold a portion of spiritual karma, and this is what will help the soul to review and to have a destination. A person adds to the handbook each day of their life. I will explain. The human will come with a destination, and a person to share the game with. In most cases the souls begin to follow the parent, their advisor, and what humans call wisdom. The child or adult, depending on the time, might feel a pulling from within their soul. This is the spirit around them telling them to listen to their soul and to remember the rules. The outer soul will begin to take on what they remember from past lives or even what they see around them. Together with this, they store it in the mind and give the information to the inner soul. This will build human karma. The human karma or society's handbook is human garbage. When a person says that their life is going in the wrong direction, or they cannot figure out why they are not happy, it has a lot to do with this. Please remember you are a free spirit, even here on Earth.

Let's look at some of the things that humans have added to society's handbook and hand over to others in life.

Time factor is a big one. In spiritual world there is no time. In human life you have time. Together with this you must advance and follow a time flow. Now remember, the game of life is to have fun, and to understand others and to love. When you add time to this, you are already at a disadvantage. If you are trying to keep up with a clock, you will have no time to understand another person or yourself.

Another is achievement. The soul does not need to achieve. In the spiritual world, since there is no time, the soul can learn, teach, and enjoy when it wishes with no pressure. Many humans feel that if they do not have a certain amount of material belongings or achieve a certain amount of accomplishments, they failed in life. No one can fall short in playing a game if you play to have fun.

Another factor is satisfaction. So many need to have satisfaction. I have heard people say, "I'm not fulfilled." While you play the game, love all of the game. Have adventure; allow your heart to share, and to be open. All spirit is free; this is why death is beautiful.

Many mortals take on habits. The human race watches and duplicates what is around them, whether its right or wrong, in order to have. Think about a child's board game and watch your child at play. He will imitate another if he feels that player is better, in the fear that he might lose. This is because he was taught that losing is not fun. The human soul does not like to be alone or different.

Another of society's rules is to have stress. I do not know of a human soul that does not leave the Earth's plane without stress. I think humans feel if they have stress or a disease they did it right.

Sometimes in life you will come with an ailment. This is spiritual karma. There is no need to add to it or allow stress to come into your life. It will prevent many from enjoyment. You might come into life with characteristics that another will have, but many reproduce certain character traits in the hopes to be a better player.

There are many games in life, and you choose which

one you will play and for how long. Sometimes all the
players will change and sometimes only a few. A different
game might take you to an opposite part of the world. The
change could bring joy or even tragedy in your life. You
might stay with the same game. Some might question why
different games?

Well, it is a choice, the same as in spiritual world. To live
you need freedom. It refreshes the soul. In some cases you
might have made arrangements to be with different players in a life, or be able to start life over. So many feel they
are stuck. There are some who feel they will never advance
to the next game. This can come from society's handbook.
Even though I gave you some of society's handbook, there
are many links from the ones I gave. Did you ever hear
someone say to another, "Don't give up, hang in there?" "If
you change things now it could cost you."

The soul will come to a stop and begin to shut down,
when you deny yourself to move on. Sometimes illness can
occur. There are incidents where staying put can be good.
If you know from within you are not happy, allow yourself
to know there is another game, and the next game can be
the main purpose of your life.

To play the game of life is to be yourself, and allow the
inner self to release the energy it came with. This energy
will become stronger as your life goes on. Try to imagine
yourself like a tree. If you enjoy all the games in life you
will grow, become sturdy, and you will branch out into
many different areas. As you know, most trees will live a

long time, which is what every soul wants. The soul understands that life is eternal. The soul should lead the body, and if you allow your soul to show you life, you will love your life.

When I hear a person say, "What should I be doing with my life?"

I would say the best place to get the answer is inside of you. The human race needs to stop and breathe. The world will not be destroyed, and you can never run out of what mortal's refer to as time. There is a lot to see and do, and you will not complete this in every area of life, or be with every person. But why miss yourself? Humans will feel they are on the wrong path, when they spend so little time working on themselves. Why can't we go a little deeper inside ourselves and listen to the thoughts that are given? If we listen to the thoughts and sounds inside, the road might become wider, and your life will have as much as any other person, but it will be seen in a different light. That light will not only give back to you but to others around you. That light is energy.

Try to play the game, and never feel destroyed. The regrets you feel now will be taken from you when you depart. There is no need to sit out a game or to live life depressed. The winning of the game comes from within. If you feel good about any day of your life, then you have won.

You need to understand that life is basic and simple. It is like sitting on a porch on a Sunday morning and hearing the nearby church bells and taking in the smell of fresh

flowers. When you lose control in your life, you relinquish
the soul, and that is when the subconscious mind takes
over. The game will be the main purpose of the day. This
can include many things. Perhaps you will focus mainly
on the material way of life. The basics will become foreign
to you, and so will your soul.

I have seen so many with illnesses who should be
healthy in life, yet some will never change their lives. Many
come with the idea to press on, that this life was given to
them to learn through hurt, anger, or problems. The problems that occur are telling the human that their eternal
energy needs more, that life can improve. The challenges
that will come into a life might build strength, yet it can be
a simple sign that is saying to move on. Then something
happens reminding you that you are more than just skin
and bones. This is when your soul will have its day. For
some it is only a day, but others will begin to truly live. The
soul should always walk in front of the body. This means,
having no fear. If you could only understand, you are not
here to be punished or to have sins; you are here to enjoy.
The sins you believe you have are only reminders that you
need to turn to yourself and spirit, and you will be guided.
Try to give to others. Allow them to know you. Show them
that you care, and that they are part of your game. If all
would take fifteen minutes each day to share something
with another soul, the world could change. The spiritual
soul needs to communicate and to touch. The one thing
everyone needs to understand is that we are all here to

play together. If you feel you are the only player, or need every spot, you will play alone.

What is the best way to introduce the game of life to yourself and to others? The word I would use is fun. The purpose in life is not to have everything, or to be better than the next person, or envy anyone else, but just to have enjoyment.

Now you could be thinking, I need to work, and that is not always fun. If you have a family that might bring stress and sacrifices, start with communication, say what you feel and think. The thoughts you receive are there for a reason. The emotions you feel, the voice that cries out and speaks to you. If you start with this, you are telling the other players of life, that you exist. You will be part of the game, not a person who is being pushed through the game of life. Try to learn the rules and follow them. Get to know the other players and try to understand why they play the game the way they do. If you keep landing on the same spot or to put it in different terms, in the same place in life, depressed, unhealthy, over worked, etc. ask your soul if there is a reason. That is the clue. No one is that unlucky, or is too depressed; you're just not playing the game right.

With every game, there are small cards that will move you to a different position, or that will take you back a step. In life I call this the IN'S and OUT'S. The IN'S are happenings that will come to you that can improve your life, if you take the chance. It could be a person you would meet, or maybe being taught something. It could be as simple as getting up on the right side of the bed, to a fresh day where all goes well. Sometimes we exercise these IN'S, and sometimes we let them pass. As for the OUT'S, they are just the contrast. They will help us to rest when the soul needs an adjustment. They will give a way out of that game you are playing and into another. They will also help with the ending of your life. When I say to you, "A soul adjustment," this is when the soul needs to be healed, or a long rest. You might become sick with the flu or cold. You might find yourself tired and sleeping a lot, or even injured. As to changing the game, this could be as simple as feeling good about yourself or someone else. You might feel you need a break from life and will go away or change something. When you pass over, everyone picks their time and the place when they will leave. If the soul closes down because you are not allowing the soul to totally live, it will look for a way out. It will want to return to spiritual world where it can survive and go on. With this, there could be near death experiences, a near miss car accident, etc. In most cases this will revise the soul and the body to come together and continue on with the game.

So you see life has a lot to offer, and as humans you will add many things. The one thing you need to add more is love, for love is more than an emotion; it is the connecting thread that holds the human and the spiritual life together. Every time you allow yourself to open up, and you communicate out to others, the thread becomes stronger. The body will begin to heal, and the human game will become easier for all to play. Have fun with your life, for each life is an original one, which you created. When it's over, it is over, like some feel. They are also right. You will go back, and decide whether you will recreate yourself into another life, so you can play the game again. Have fun, love, and always understand all around you.

BLINDERS

Life with Ruthie has opened many doors for myself. I have learned that the game of life is to enjoy. The ones we meet and come to know become a part of us, and teach us so we can be better players in future games. The spirit that is around you will work with you, not to do it for you, but only to help you improve your daily life.

For some there are blinders. This will happen to all of us at some stage in life. You will put on blinders, and fail to see you have one of the greatest advantages with you at all times, the spirit of your own soul, and the energy it possesses. The spirit that guides you throughout your life always walks with you. The blinders are what you choose, the same as other things in your life. When you lift the blinders and allow your soul to have a connection with spirit and yourself, you will begin to feel comfort. Why do we allow blinders to come to us, and who offers the blinders to us? It is not evil in any way. They are one of the OUT'S in a mortal life. As we have mentioned before, the game of life has IN'S and OUT'S. The IN'S are the opportunity to go forward, and view each open door. The OUT'S are when we choose to close down and wait. Without using our own energy, we block out life and hope for solutions.

When we look at the world around us and see the conflict and unhappiness, yet we go on with our daily agenda and feel it will improve, these are blinders. The world, as Ruthie has said, is a gift to use, to enjoy, and to love. To do this you need to understand all that is around you. You need to know that you can go on and have a good life. It's not hard work, but it is a job.

Ruthie has taught me to look into my soul, and investigate my emotions and traits. When you look at others and their lives, look past the skin and see the soul. Their skin, race, and religious beliefs might not be the same as yours, but their souls are. For they too hunger for love and peace. Take time to listen, and view their game in life as you will view your own. Life is important to all and they are part of your energy, you will see this in spiritual world. They have the right to show their special gifts to the world, and we need to learn to appreciate them.

As children we are full of love and understanding. A child will question what they do not understand and look for an answer. As adults we play the game of life to win only. As a mortal you never look around and communicate why you have that need. Could it be a part of greed that is in all mankind? A mortal will want to own and possess. In reality all that surrounds you is on loan. If you feel you have ownership you will not give of yourself or take time to notice life. The world is the game board for all to play with. You are the players. Your bodies are the game pieces that you move around. The game of life is fair. There are reasons and answers for every move you make, and you are the one who makes the moves. If you feel life is unfair, whether it be in health, emotions, character, talent, or money, you need to change games or even players. A form of love means to move forward and seek. The soul under your skin is pure energy that needs movement. This is why you have a brain and a memory. Never measure your life by a clock or possessions for this is a sign of ownership, and you will miss the fun of life. Look at greed and work on taking it out of your game. Many look at greed as being a person who will not share or give. There are different forms of greed in the world today. You can have greed of yourself, never opening up to another. There are times when a mortal will play so hard at the game, that they never see the other players. Look at the things you do in a course of a day. See how many can be related to the word greed. It could be as simple as preventing love to come to you or others.

In spiritual world there are families. Each family member will nourish each other. This makes the energy that they share strong, and the love and understanding shows through. The world needs to come together as a family, and work with the energy they receive from spirit. The greed of the world needs to take a back seat to love.

Love seems like a simple word, yet it has various meanings. For some, love can be a reaction that gives hurt, and that hurt can scar a person for life. There are some that will go through life searching and searching for what they sense love should be, but will never find it. This word is used in many different ways and for many purposes, it is a healing, and can be an obstacle. The inner voice calls for love even in the person that seems ruthless; they too need and want love. The meaning of love is three words-Hope, Affection, and Patience. When you have hope you use that ability to seek out the love that soul has to offer, and carry no fear in your own soul. The word Affection means you want to give love the way you want to receive love back. Third is patience for love is timeless, there is no need to rush love, or feel you will never find love. The eternal love that we all share needs to be brought forward and shown each moment of the day. The soul can be fooled by love, but if a person is willing to bypass the foolish moment and realize that all love is not foolish. We must never stop love just because we were hurt, the hurt will heal, and we must understand that love is more than a moment, it is eternal.

RUTHIE'S WORDS

A human life is a simple life. All humans come with all of the energy and power they need to complete and to enjoy their life. I call this your spot. We as spirits give an extra gift to life, the guidance of love and understanding. It is not always easy in life to see where you are headed and have full understanding of all your decisions. Sometimes it will take a lifetime to see what is in front of you. This does not mean you missed out on your life, only that you chose a path that was longer.

In some cases it is hard for some to believe in spirit or God's energy. This is not a sin, nor should that person feel that they are less. We all choose a path that we feel is right at that moment in time. For all are correct. Whatever you believe in is what fills your heart and soul. A mortal needs to share their energy no matter what their skin characteristics are. This love that we share, which might show through as hate, will draw us together. You do not repeat a life until you get it right. You return to share, and to be able to select whatever you choose. If you put your life on hold hoping to find perfection, you will miss out on all the fun life has to offer. The one thing so many want and need in life is peace. The human will spend hours trying to find out how to achieve this. Peace is you. You need to express yourself and not have fear.

What is life?

Life is like a day in a child's life. The child will awaken not sure what the day will hold for them. Only that they are happy and alive. They will take on whatever comes their way. Whether they go out to play or stay in, they will look for opportunities. While at play they are able to use all of their imagination, and experiment with new things. They will have some hurts, but they will recover. They will have adventures, and they will search and find new things to interest them. They will share with friends and have secrets. They will take time to learn and to teach others around them, and most of all have the ability to have fun at all they choose. They will never hold back or have fear of showing emotions. If they fall down, they are willing to stand again. If they do not understand, they will seek the answers. The soul of a child is honest and loyal. They have faith in all. There is never a problem with sharing. They show their true soul from the inside out. They can find happiness in the smallest of things. They will give love to all and never question why. Their skin is theirs only to soil, religion is their belief, and their mind is their tool.

The most important thing is that they never feel alone. They know a parent, animal, or even an imaginary friend named spirit, who is close by loves them.

As for death, it is also like a day in a child's life. When the day comes to an end, the child will be called in. Someone who loves them will greet them and care for them. They will take in nutriments to give them back the energy they lost playing. They will share the stories of the day and take a deep breath. They will be cleansed thoroughly. They will rest until sleep comes to them, knowing that tomorrow is another day, and they will awaken and go out to play once again.

To me, life and death are actually as simple as a day in a child's life. It's filled with love, understanding, and fun.

With this I bid you good day.

Love
Ruthie

QUICK ORDER FORM

Fax Orders – 609-586-0469
Email orders – ruthieandliz1354@yahoo.com
Postal Orders – P. O. Box 271 Yardley, PA 19067
Web Site – www.ruthiewisdom.com

Please send me more free information on:

- Speaking/Seminars
- Newsletters
- Readings

Name:	
Address:	
City:	
State:	Zip:
Telephone:	
Work:	
Home:	
Cell:	
Email address:	

Shipping: US $4.00 for first book and $2.00 for each additional book.
International: $9.00 for first book and $5.00 for each additional book. (Estimate).
Payment: Check or Money order (DO NOT SEND CASH)

Printed in the United States
by Baker & Taylor Publisher Services